ISBN-10: 1979744041

ISBN-13: 978-1979744041

Published by Civin Media Relations

www.civinmediarelations.com

Printed in the United States

Amazon Create Space

Available at www.acupofkindnessbothel.com

Dedication

This book is dedicated to all the beautiful children of the world. You are our hope for unity in a world divided by differences. We need to change. Be the change.

"Sometimes it is the people no one imagines anything of, who do the things that no one can imagine"-Alan Touring

~ Beca

If kindness came from coffee beans,
I'd enjoy a cup each day.
Drive right down to the coffee stand,
Sip a cup of large gourmet.

The aroma would be so heavenly,
With a flavor you can't resist.
And though it seems this can't be true,
Such a place just may exist.

In a city whose name is Bothell,
A modern Eden some would say.
Comes a story like a fairy tale,
In a cobalt blue café.

By an Arco in the great Northwest,
Country's coffee brewing mecca.
There's a drive thru stand about 6 by 9,
And a barista whose name is Beca.

She's as tiny as her coffee stand; some might say they're both pint-sized.
But if you measured Beca's heart, we know you'd be surprised.

"Treat everyone with kindness, and there's no way you could lose."
A gourmet cup at a bargain price, is the essence Beca brews.

Folks drive miles for fresh fruit teas,
Or a mocha with Salted Carmel Toffee.
And all who visit Beca's Brew,
Leave with so much more than coffee.

On a warm spring day in Bothell,
Beca spotted a lonely man.
Invited him over; introduced herself,
And their friendship soon began.

"Hey, guess what? My name is Will. Do you wanna hear a joke?"
Beca showed the kindness many don't, and listened closely as he spoke.

Will faces special challenges, but what makes him so unique.
Is his happiness, joy & zest for life through each sentence that he speaks.

"I'll make a deal", said Beca.
"Come visit me each day.
We'll enjoy a drink, and share some laughs,
And pass the time away."

Their friendship soon developed,
Through their positive attitudes.
He became a part of Beca's place,
Like the coffee that she brews.

"You're my very best friend, right Beca?"
A common phrase that he would say.
"Bye, Beca. I love you."
Is how he ends their day.

Beca recognized the good in Will,
Through a heart that's pure and true.
They'd spend each day together,
As their friendship grew and grew.

One day a woman came to the stand, ordered a coffee hot and black.
She treated Will so poorly, Beca told her, "Don't come back."

She looked at Will with sadness.
What kind of message did she send?
Even though she lost a customer,
she must do that for her friend.

Soon Beca learned of his birthday,

He would be thirty-one.

She wanted to throw Will a party,

But would Bothell really come?

A Cup of Kindness

She posted on a neighborhood blog,
A great plan she would devise.
Invited the city to Beca's Brew.
To throw Will a surprise.

The community came out by the dozens,
As Beca hoped they would.
An event that will be talked about,
Where the whole world seems so good.

A ride around Bothell with the men in blue
Filled Will to the brim with pleasure.
But what they gave to Will that day,
Is a love you cannot measure.

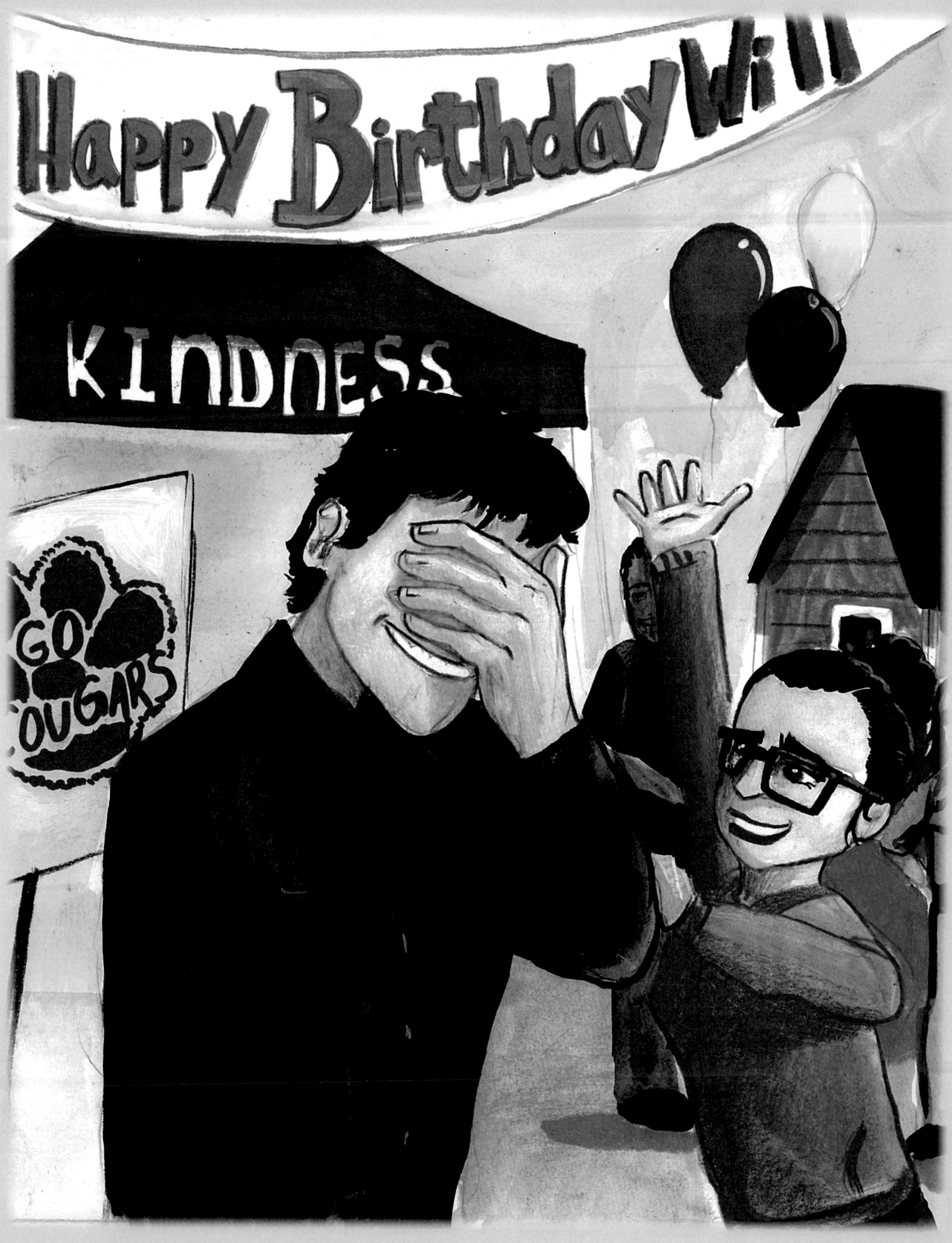
Happy Birthday Will
KINDNESS
GO COUGARS

Eric's Heroes shared the story; showed Will's birthday far and wide.
Giving millions the opportunity to feel the warmth inside.

Will was overwhelmed at first. A day he hoped would never end.
Greater than the gifts that he received, were his new amount of friends.

As you wake for school this morning,
And another day begins.
Remember that every person matters
And kindness always wins.

A Word from the Author

I wrote this book with the hope that it may teach children everywhere to not only be kind, but also accepting. Differences are not meant to divide people but unite them. How could we learn to grow if we surrounded ourselves only with people of the same likeness? We can't.

You can learn so much from your neighbor if you just took the time to get to know them. Today we live in such a world of uncertainty that is fueled by hatred of anyone that is different . This has to stop. We must, as a people, no matter race, sex, religion or ethnicity, stand united. If we want a better future for our children, it needs to start today.

If we all just did one act of kindness to one person each day, could you imagine the positive impact it would make on the world? Just one. I'm starting with me because if I want change, I must be that change. Maybe, just maybe, that's all it would take. Because even the smallest grain of rice, can tip a scale.

The next time you meet someone that is different from you, I hope you take a moment to remember that every person matters and kindness always wins.

Love, Beca

---

1. As you read through the book, pay attention to little details. The word "kindness" is hidden somewhere on each page. (To show children that kindness is all around us if we just take a moment to look.)

2. When reading with children here are some thought provoking questions to engage them.

    a) Why was Will being ignored?

    b) Is that something that you would do to someone?

    c) Look around you. Don't we all look different?

    d) Just because you're different does that mean you can't be friends?

    e) Why did Beca ask the lady to leave? Would you do the same for your friend?

    f) How do you think Will felt when so many people came out to celebrate his birthday?

    g) Has anyone surprised you before? How did that make you feel?

    h) Because Beca was kind to Will, he was able to gain many new friends. What if we all did that? Wouldn't the world be better?

Acknowledgements

This book wouldn't have been possible without the village of people who have loved and supported me along the way.

To the incomparable City of Bothell: Thank you for not only supporting me, but for embracing me since day one. This community is filled with so many amazing people who sprinkle kindness everywhere they go. You are inspiring millions of communities across the world to show love and kindness to everyone. You guys rock!!

To the "Golden Heart" of this city, the Bothell Police Department: Thank you. Every single day you serve and protect this city. That goes beyond the call of duty. I can't thank you enough for always keeping an eye on my stand and for not hesitating to call me when I'm not there. Sheriff Cummings: I don't know what you're putting in their donuts but it's working. Keep up the good work. It doesn't go unnoticed.

To my KOMO 4 family: I'm speechless. You told our story and it was simply beautiful. Eric, Joan, Doug and Darrin: Thank you for taking the time to develop the story and to really get to know Will and I. You helped spread a message that is so much bigger than the video and has spread like wild fire across the world. You are journalism at its finest.

To Civin Media and Publishing: Thank you for giving me the opportunity to publish a book with such a beautiful message. Todd, thank you for being my co-author and publisher. Never once did you show frustration with my "micro-managing and my perfectionist ways." You allowed me to share this story and you allowed me to do it my way. You are not only my publisher but my friend.

To my artist Jason: You are simply amazing. Your artistic ability to put into detail a place you have never been to is genius. You took on this project because you believed in the message of kindness. Thank you.

Tammi: Thank you for all that you are. You wear so many hats, you could fill a boutique. You are inspiring.

Thank you Kathy at Yard Announcements. Your beautiful displays have gone beyond Will's birthday to help spread the message of kindness. You wholeheartedly love doing it and I am so grateful for you.

To my family and friends: Without your continued love and support I wouldn't be at this place in my journey. Thank you and I love you all.

Mom and Dad: I can't begin to express the gratitude and admiration I have for you both. The morals, values and spiritual faith that was instilled in me at a young age has shaped me into the person I am today. Thank you.

To my greatest joy, Bella: You are my perfect blessing from God. While I have been teaching you about life, you have been showing me the true meaning of life. Mommy loves you so much, Princess.

To my dearest Willy: Some people search a lifetime to find the friend for their soul. I'm so lucky I didn't have to search long. Your heart is pure and loyal and has inspired millions from all walks of life to be more like you. Our friendship has taught me lessons that I can share with others. That is priceless. Your light shows people God's love. Thank you. I love you, buddy and I will always be right by your side.

With love and gratitude,

Beca

73081169R10020

Made in the USA
Lexington, KY
07 December 2017

"But how would you have known that in reality, it was a bunch of people remembering how good it feels to take part in another human being's happiness? Someone who's heart is pure and true."

Eric Johnson KOMO 4 News

ISBN 9781979744041

90000 >

9 781979 744041

Puzzles Works Book

Math Beginning ematics

Visual Multiplication

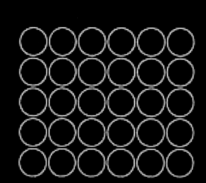

_____ rows and

_____ columns

makes a total of

_____

_____ rows and

_____ columns

makes a total of

_____